W9-ADG-895

BLACK BOX

BOOKS BY FRANK X WALKER

Affrilachia

Buffalo Dance: The Journey of York

BLACK BOX

poems by

FRANK X WALKER

OLD COVE PRESS

LEXINGTON, KENTUCKY 2006

Published by
OLD COVE PRESS
P.O. Box 22886
Lexington, Kentucky 40522
www.oldcovepress.com

Composed in Minion
Prepress services by Beau Graphics, Lexington
Printed and bound by CJK, Cincinnati
Printed on Finch Opaque Vellum

Old Cove Press thanks
Anne N. Bornschein, Francie Chassen-Lopez, Tracy A. Hawkins,
Lori-Lyn Hurley, Pat Latham, Michaele Pride-Wells and Denise Smith
for important assistance in making this book.

ISBN 0-9675424-1-3

Printed in the U.S.A.

Publisher's Cataloging-in-Publication Data
Walker, Frank X
Black box / poems by Frank X Walker.
Lexington, KY: Old Cove Press, 2006.
p. cm.
ISBN 0-9675424-1-3
1. Afro-Americans–Kentucky–Poetry. I. Title

FIRST EDITION

for Faith A. Smith and Alan Walker Chiles
alpha and omega

Special thanks to the Lannan Foundation, the Affrilachian Poets, my Cave Canem family, my Zeta Phi Beta Sigma family, my Spalding family, the Walker and Warner clans, Nikki, Dvan, Kenneth, Michaele, Tracy, Gurney Norman, and the eyes, hands and heart of Nyoka Hawkins. This child belongs to us.
— Frank X Walker
Lexington, Kentucky

Contents

Black Box

Kentucky vs. Texas Western, 1966

On our side of the tracks
that game
cast a shadow as luminous
as Joe Louis' gloves
raised upright, like corn stalks
like rockets, like Jesse Owens
on the gold medal stand in Berlin

I see Daddy and Flick, a skinny would-be point guard
an even skinnier coulda been forward
ace boons from way back
closer than brothers
since they could pee straight, skip school
balance filter cigarettes like fireflies
in alleys and parking lots
like traveling magicians at a two-penny carnival

I see them huddled around
a smoldering potbellied stove of a radio
still salty
from frayed leather prayers launched
toward the crooked rim
on the side of the tobacco barn
hearts pumping, muscles ready and loose
they saddle themselves aboard
every broadcasted syllable like neon jockeys
as much a part of the audience as every ticket-holder
in the arena

As much to lose as
the five black faces on the floor and
more than any body on the bench
a two-headed pep band
flat-chested cheerleaders, unable to sit
they slap palms and knuckle up
they black hand sides, wager the value of their
manhood on the final score
like so many more
black and country boys and men
whose only connection to the pages in my history books
floated on AM dials and radio waves
rare television footage
that imported two-dimensional
black and white and flaming images
of Birmingham, D.C. and Watts
into quiet country towns
in middle America
Danvilles, Harrodsburgs, Perryville battlefields
reveling in segregated comfort zones
propped up by traditions as rigid as back doors
and rebel flags

It was not just a game, *rebound*
it was evidence that the un-civil war, *pass*
not only could be won, *dribble*
but they, though young, country and black ... *shoot*
were not alone ... *swish!*

Handmade

for David Russell Walker

granddaddy's hands, like tree limbs
with the bark peeled off
were not dry and brittle
but strong and supple
polished mahogany when
chopping and hauling wood
for mamma e's kitchen stove

quick and decisive
when wringing a chicken's neck
to feed his family
they stopped shaking when he
dipped into a can of prince albert tobacco
removing a perfect pinch
and rolled a filterless cigarette
while waiting for the sun to join him
on the job or in the field

thumbs as big and hard as hammerheads
five-inch nails for fingers
he built wood frame houses
limestone fences and sturdy lives
hands too busy to commit his life to books
he married a teacher
and learned how much he already knew
from living simply
the rest he would teach himself

granddaddy dave rarely turned a page
but could cipher, sight and measure
with his black knotty slide rule
elbow to finger
  two feet
heel to toe
  twelve inches

every door he built for us
was designed without locks
was as high as he could reach
and he was grandfather tall

though not perfect
he glued, stapled and hammered together
a mother load of fractured promises
sanded smooth many a rough edge
with even rougher hands
and tried to set things right
all the way to the end

Canning Memories

Indian summer Saturday mornings
meant project door screens sat open
waiting for the vegetable truck

No new moons or first frosts
just the horn on an old flatbed
trumpeting the harvest

No almanac announcement, no ads
just a short black farmer in overalls
and mud-caked boots

Grandmothers who still clicked
their tongues, who called up the sound
of a tractor at daybreak
the perfume of fresh turned earth
and the secret location of the best
blackberry patch
like they were remembering
old lovers, planted themselves
a squint away from palming
and weighing potatoes
string beans, kale, turnips, sweet corn
onions and cabbage

They seeded themselves
close enough to see each other
bent low in the fields, pulling weeds

dispensing verbal insecticide
gingham dresses gathered in front
cradling cucumbers and Big Boy tomatoes
destined for kitchen windowsills
and mason jars

They break sacred ground far away
from these acres of red brick
and concrete neighbors
close enough to the earth
to know
    if all city folk plant iz family 'n friends
    alls dey gonna gets iz funerals

View Finder
for William Warner, Sr.

In the photo
only suspenders, a black leather belt
and the shadow under a hat
are darker than your face,
a charcoal reservoir for the sun

A hand-rolled filterless cigarette dances
at the edge of your smile
like a ghost
The child cradled at your hip
is wringing her tiny hands
unable to look away to the camera
She is only four
but she recognizes the smell of the devil
on your lips

Acres and acres of your life
hang from the top rails
inside the tobacco barn
This is supposed to be a victory photo
so you allow yourself the pleasure
of a special blend
savoring the raw strength
of its unknown toxins

Next to you
in my father's arms
my entire hand gripping the expanse
of his thumb
I am fully focused
on the mysterious blinking eye

Kodak Moment

When I was eight
Mamma told me between sobs
that he went out one night
and lost himself between some sheets
that he fell down
and didn't get back up
fast enough
that he was never coming home
Then she told her mamma
over the phone
that she kicked his ass out
for masquerading as a man

She wouldn't look at old photographs
She burned all the ones
she couldn't cut in half

She never knew
I kept an out of focus black and white
of the three of us
in the bottom of my underwear drawer
next to the last bar of his
Lucky Heart soap

Photosynthesis

My body takes photographs
that show up on my skin
as scars
intaglio etchings
organic polaroids
that remind me
of my almost tragic youth

My skin remembers
the long rusty nail
peeking through the top
of my bare left foot
the argument the hot bacon grease
had with the wet potatoes
the handshake with the wrong end of the iron

These scars stand as reminders
to avoid razor-sharp objects
white-hot metal and pear-scented sheets

No matter how hard I try
or how easily I forget
my skin
always
remembers

Family Reunion

I remember the first time
Mamma's body swoll up and up
until something like water broke
and they took her away
breathing like the fat boy
we chased all the way home
from school

She come home shrunk near back
to normal, looking tired
walking tender and toting a new
store-bought blanket
close to her chest

I thought little sisters and brothers
arrived in pink or blue blankets
until the summer I sat down at a picnic table
across from a shorter image of me

We drank the same pop
skinned our chicken parts
picked the onions
out of our baked beans
and found out our daddies
had the same name

Glutton

I could barely lift the slop buckets
we kept in the house
on account of stray dogs
and bored teenagers

After collecting contributions
from neighbors in exchange for
false promises
of a foot or a ham
come Christmas
I would ride in the back
of a pickup truck with the slop
all the way to Davistown
where Mamma's second husband
housed a litter of pigs

They squealed and gobbled down
corn cobs, potato peelings
apple cores, moldy bread, chicken bones
hard cheese, orange rinds and burnt toast

Like him
they didn't need to hear Mamma say amen
to start eating
and they wouldn't stop
until everything was gone

Watching them grow fat and slow
and mean
didn't increase my appetite
for pork chops, bacon or fathers

I was too soft
to be a real farmer, he said
and I'd better keep my head
in them books
or learn to starve
when I became a man

Sugar Babies

We learned to covet
from a man who kept sweets
a guitar and comic books
hidden away
in a metal locker
in the corner of the master bedroom

Once I learned to trick the door
my strong fingers
and my sisters' bony wrists
became the raiding party
that would take all but one
of his favorite cookies
and occasionally smash his
personal loaf of bread

A man and a lock taught us
how to covet
When we escaped with booty
we taught ourselves to share

The crumbs we ate
were our small victory
but sugar, music and heroes
became the things
we wanted most

Twenty-First Sentry

I look up when heads bow
turn into a doberman
when everybody kneels to pray
shoulders straight
eyes at attention
I don't blink
not even for a second
sweeping the room with searchlights
on high beam
until someone says amen

It's not out of disrespect
or lack of fear
It's just that somebody's
got to stand guard
so I do
like back then
before the divorce
when I discovered my mother's
husband tipping down the hall
to my sister's room
late at night
when every eye was shut
but mine

So I stand here
eyes wide open
jaws locked

muscles coiled
waiting to catch anyone
with preying
on his mind

Writes of Passage

Nez Percé boys go hunting or fishing
for salmon or trout
The Zulu sent Chaka
into the wild to find a lion
My tribe sent me down the gauntlet
that was the aisle of a yellow bus
the first week of senior high

Every red, white and blue Converse high-top
step was punctuated
with double slaps to the hook of my head
or quick kicks to the back of my knees

I carried a nerd load of books and teared up
way too fast to become one of them but
excommunication was its own reward

I learned to enjoy the solitude and long walks
to class, where I polished up the angry young
couplets I wrote in my head
and tried to understand the square root
of meanness

How many cultures choose their griots
their shamans, their poets
by putting them off the bus?

Too Wise Men

My earliest inclinations
were way too secular for membership
in the House of God youth choir
At twelve, I was bound for hell
and the Little League
but if Mamma needed an extra angel
wise man or an emergency Joseph
she'd flip her old Singer to the upright position
scrape together enough thread
and a yard or two of old curtains and sheets
trusting that I knew all the words
just 'cause I lived in her house
and she played the Temptations'
Christmas album around the clock
as soon as the Thanksgiving turkey
was hash

I didn't know frankincense from myrrh
still don't, but I learned to balance
a crooked metal halo, make up
my own words to 'Silent Night'
and stop asking how a baby boy
born that close to Africa
to such ordinary folks
could grow up to be so   white

Elves

for Helen Ewing

Santa couldn't come
until my fingers and arms ached
from cutting up raisins and walnuts
after carrying blackberry jam
flour, sugar and eggs
wax paper, vanilla
and boxes of Duncan Hines
all the way home
from the A&P uptown

until Rudolph, Frosty
the Grinch, the Little Drummer Boy
and the Nutcracker
danced across the screen
and the smell of tangerines
and the last jam cake
overpowered
the fresh-cut pine in the air

until Aunt Helen put on her lipstick
Avon perfume
her good wig
and stood in the screen door, waiting
for the shadowy figures
to drop off toys
and stay awhile

he couldn't come
until Mamma teased me
out of my slumber
and sent me tipping through the snow
door to door
armed with screwdrivers
wrenches and extra batteries
in case somebody else's daddy
forgot

Altitude Adjustment

We all made fun
of little sawed-off Sylvia Horton
taking privileges with her name
while rewriting Dr. Seuss
snickering at the way she dressed
like somebody's granny
long skirts, no makeup, dead hair
plain shoes

Seemed odd for a fifth-grade girl
to not smell like bubblegum
or wear pigtails
as odd as the large scarlet birthmark
that dominated her globe of a face
like Europe and Asia combined

I remember my own face
when the Salvation Army Christmas
toy and food deliverers
emptied their arms and boxes
and erased the empty space
beneath our crooked tree

Every mean thing I ever did
every unkind word
returned like a fist to my throat

then rained down my face
in tiny beads of sweat
when my mother made us hug
our benefactors, Sylvia first

Afterward, I watched her grow tall
in our silence

Enough

I remember tying up dirty clothes
in bed sheets to be transported
to the laundromat across town
in a yellow cab

I remember large block letters
on plain white boxes and cans
and discovering that USDA peanut butter
was not as smooth or creamy as the neighbor's Jif

Before free lunch and food stamps
we could leave school at noon to eat
Sometimes we would split a fried-egg sandwich
Sometimes we would have a long walk home

Summers were spent under the bed
shirtless and reading, stuck to the cool tile floor
Government housing
didn't come with air-conditioning

I remember quietly disappearing and running
home and away from the sound
of the ice cream man
before we learned to pour red Kool-Aid
into ice-tray Popsicle treats

Other kids always had more house
more toys, more food, more daddies

but Mamma said we were rich
'cause we always had
enough

Jesuit
for the Danville Admirals

Coach had a hard time
convincing me that
someone on the other team
had done something so horrendous
I was supposed to strap on my chin strap
wade into the thick of battle
intent on doing bodily harm

Best I could do
was wait until somebody rang my bell
threw a chop block
or caught me off guard
with a cheap shot
Then, my violence was simply
a matter of self-defense

Mamma's turn-the-other-cheek philosophy
didn't go over well
with Coach Swain
and he was a Bible scholar, too
always ranting about David and Goliath
and what Joshua did at Jericho

If we needed the fire and brimstone
at halftime
he'd wade through the valley
of our hung heads

conjure up the image of Moses
and the powerful Red Sea
smiting ol' Pharaoh's army
Then he'd get in everyone's face
yelling and spitting
sometimes losing his partial plate
in the process

As soon as we returned to the field
I'd catch a glimpse
of the smooth-legged Delilahs
in short skirts and pom-poms
close my eyes
and try to find the Samson in me

Curiosity

She lay there calmly
smiling quietly
chewing her Juicy Fruit
snapping it in my ear

Two large ruby nipples
almost no breasts
she moved her hips twice
I quivered once
bumping my head
on the steering wheel

I offered her eleven dollars
and some change
She just smiled
and patted me on the head

Why We Keep Plants

Carnival goldfish and guppies
that survived the weekend
were finished off with generous portions
of self-rising cornmeal
and too much attention
from the many hands and eyes
of my younger siblings

The tiny aquarium
became a planter
after its bloated floating contents
circled the bowl twice
and disappeared

Jim Dandy, more racehorse than mouse
escaped from the cardboard box
but not the neighbor's fear or feet

We buried him out back
shrouded in notebook paper
resting in an empty
Quaker Oats container
his last rites shifted
to a plot for revenge
that somehow dried all the tears

Pepper, way too curious to be content
in our makeshift doghouse
had been missing for a day
when I recognized the fluff of hair
dancing on the double-yellow line
in the middle of Lexington Road

Risking the same fate
I used a crushed soda can
to scrape up what was left
and told my sisters
he ran away

Frontier Spirit

Out of respect for the lake
and the rules, my inner tube
remained tied to the mooring,
my glasses to my face,
then one a them Johnson boys
each trying to outbrave the other
began to drift away
carried by a passing speedboat's wave
that bounced off the bank
rocking the wooden dock
throwing us about like crumbs
of bread
then lil' Jimmy forgot
we couldn't swim

When his hand came up
for a second grab at air
I was stretching my own tubing
toward him
with little regard for rule number one

On the third try
he found my circle of life
snatched it from my grip
and clung to it
like a baby possum

The lifeguard's pursuit of the perfect tan
was interrupted
by the sounds of a second boy
drowning, so she pulled
me from the brink
before I could swallow it all

They voted me camper of the week
awarded me a plaster Daniel Boone
which we all thought was oak
until the thunderstorm
kited the living room curtain
and sent it crashing to the floor

Creek Philosophy

Mamma turned us out of doors
to discover what it means to be human
My search led me off the asphalt
down the narrow
worn path to the creek
where I studied with the master
learning to recognize what I would come to
know as resilience
while experiencing the humility
of my failed attempts to stop the flow
of water with dumb round stones

Even my perceived ability to direct
its steady current proved more
a lesson in cooperation than control

Skipping rocks came to represent
what the delicate surface of water
had to say about deflecting hard times
and even harder people
until they were slow and heavy
enough to just let go of

I grew to understand that if I could hear
the individual voices
in the heavy percussion
of water
falling

then I would see my heart beat
feel the blood
in my own creeks when
I made a fist
and eventually come to know
the difference between
being heavy in the world
and knowing peace

Salt

After the balloons are released
they palm shiny new diplomas
turn tassels and toast
their long-awaited independence

They quick-hug tired mothers
in Sunday dresses
leave them standing waiting for photos, waiting
for credit deserved, for validation
for the pomp and circumstance for graduating
them out of the streets at night
and out of bed every morning for twelve lonely years

Combing the crowd
they search the ocean of well-wishers
like lifeguards, looking for lost smiles
for namesakes, for fathers floating
for mermen to break the surface
not another promise

Spirits damp
they follow maternal lighthouses back to shore
leaving salty father wishes tangled in seaweed
discarded like driftwood
like one more empty plastic heart

Last Words

words and hugs
were not my daddy's tools
life was about work
hands were made to think

he communicated like his father
silently erecting monuments of
    pauses
even his gestures had commas

in his private workshop
behind a wall of resurrected TV sets
and engine parts
collected from the side of the road
he spent his spare time
polishing granddaddy's old saws
chisels and hammers
reconstructing assorted junk and found objects
into miniature antique furniture
and scale models of his dreams

just piddlin', he'd say
deflecting accusations
of creating something beautiful

no one ever called this man
an artist
no book spine whispers his name
yet every time I open my mouth
I can hear him sing

Earthmen

I'm a grandfather now
seeking my place in a grove of trees
a row of earthmen
honest to goodness real black farmers
who handed me a mason jar
pointed up at the night sky and stars and said
they's all lightnin' bugs boy
go catch all ya can

They picked up where absentee fathers
left off, scooping up grandsons and nephews
not leaving it up to chance
or to books or *t'womens*

A tadpole gonna be a frog
just like pigs grow up to be bacon
but boys can't no mo' get t'manhood alone
than t'bacca can cut itself
get up and walk to the barn

Lil' League Shaman
for my boy D.

Trapped in awkward bodies
powered by sugar and youth
they chase a round leather ball
up and down the hardwood at recess speed
slowed only by the shrill bleat
of a volunteer referee's whistle
or the frantic arm-waving
of hoarse frustrated coaches

My own charge, a powerless forward
approaches the game like a priest
physically able but spiritually incapable
of fighting for loose balls
engaging in body checks or hard fouls
He is technically sound but chronically
unselfish and more than content to hold
the ball when challenged

Operating under the assumption
that shooting is an art form
best approached
like t'ai chi or yoga
he visualizes the trajectory
and its final destination

In a game where speed, agility
and a burning desire to win
are coveted tools
he is as aggressive as a butterfly
and utterly amazed
at the collective effort
expended for so few points
while silently conducting his experiments
to control the direction and velocity
of the ball
by simply   breathing

Jumpman
Twentieth anniversary of Air Jordans

Mars Blackman was wrong
it was never just the shoes
never just a box of assembled-in-Asia
artificial fabric and rubber hype with insoles

With the same passion others collected
model trains, rookie cards and comic books
we have coveted your shoeboxes
stacked them in our closets like bars of gold

For twenty frantic seasons of Final Fours
we've adorned our backs with Carolina blue
named our sons Jordan, desired to deserve
to wear number twenty-three, just like you

Shiny and black, tongue wagging, fingers splayed
you stopped hiding your long limbs
unfolded yourself
heart full of nothing but air
tested the breeze then took off
from behind the free-throw line

Eclipsing my father's floating stinging butterfly
leaving the ground indefinitely, with such ease
defying gravity, achieving that now emblematic
midair wingless form, an icon etched into our
minds, souls and wallets

From hard dirt courts in Kentucky
to Lakeshore concrete playgrounds
we knew the secret to your power was something real
as real as our own hopes and dreams
something familiar, something we could touch

Now we know, it was never just the shoes
You remained head and shoulders above the fray
because you were standing on Satchel Paige
Jack Johnson, Arthur Ashe, Althea Gibson
Wilma Rudolph, Bill Russell and Jim Brown

All this time, you were standing on us

Teed Off

He hugs his father
but won't embrace himself
for fear of distancing sponsors seeking
someone safe to parade
around private plantations
with rolling greens
and 'whites only' signs

Carnivorous feline or
just another big game prize
poached and coached
raised in captivity
trained not to bite
the Masters?

But one more chicken joke
in the clubhouse
might make him ignore his home training
forget his marketing strategy
become another six-hundred-pound white tiger
in Vegas, smiling at the camera
green jacket shreds stuck
in his teeth

Nosotros

escúchame amigo
I used to be you
raking, cleaning
picking, mucking, shining
grinning, dreaming
almost invisible
to the people you serve

mis vatos
I used to be you
in the back corner of the classroom
engulfed in your own silence
waiting patiently for the curriculum
to acknowledge your existence
outside of your único día, your
cinco de mayo
to raise you above a stereotype
to speak to you with your own tongue

hermanas bonitas
I used to be you
attempting to hide behind oppressive
accents and grammar rules
surrendering to the Gap
settling for color-lessness
after discovering invisibility is imposible
and peroxide and French perfume
won't hide the Río Bravo in your smile

mi gente
somos lo mismo tú y yo
necesito decirte
cherish who you are y tu familia
ama el café of your eyes
love your nose and face
learn from my mistakes

Double Exposure

Picture me, harvesting the light
in a senior-class photo circa 1979
faux marina background
borrowed pin-striped suit
new white tie with a Windsor knot
riding my neck like a noose
Mamma's beautiful nose building a house
on my face
'black Chinese' eyes, older than me
a brave little Afro
the future and teeth as bright as the sun

In today's self-portrait, an image tinted by
a quarter-century and more mistakes,
salt-and-pepper survivors
circle like covered wagons
around the prisoners my smiles have become

Twenty-five more years like these
and my mahogany cheek bones
will be as wooden and stoic as a Dogon mask

Rustlin'
for d'ville, cincy, et al.

rustlin'
is the sound baggy jeans make
when young urban men
reach for wallets
CDs, registration or rolling papers

but rustlin' is a crime
in the wild wild west, end
or the deep south, side

rustlin' in thugged-out posses
of two or more
can cause funnel clouds
and vigilantes to form
in inner cities and barrios

they come wilding through the hood
touching down on street corners
and juke joint parking lots
lights flashing
badges glistening
in search of brazen sixteen-year-olds
with sagging baggy jeans
who refuse to bow their heads
give respect or be afraid

born-guilty rustlers
can't dodge thunder and lightning
gunpowder or the blame
as they jerk and twitch and bleed
while those sworn to protect and serve
empty their clips and reload
empty their clips and reload
'til the only sound and color is   chalk

We Real Crunk
after Gwendolyn Brooks

We real Crunk. We
Buy junk. We

Walk slow. Wear
Pants low. We

Sling rocks. Run
From cops. We

Get laid. Die
From AIDS.

Brer Fox

My brother dodged bullets
beat the pipe
is always on probation
for misdemeanors
tied his magic money clip
to all our pockets
could and would sing and dance
but only for gin and cigarettes
crowned himself prince
and treated all the whores
like queens

He thinks he's got a rabbit's foot
but he's just lucky
he's got a mamma
who prays a lot

Cold Still
for my family on the inside

giant steel doors creak
slide and lock
silence echoes down empty fluorescent
corridors
I rub my hands together
researching my own guilt
as I recognize my inability to distinguish
the chill in the air
from my fear
from my loathing

unk caught a dime and a half
cousin dookie did a nickel twice
baby brotha, a frequent felon
struck out last time
and is now pumping iron
in the belly
of one of these twenty-first-century Amistads
upstate
downriver

last night
in a basement chapel
sharing poetry and praise
with the residents of the men's
federal prison system
I looked into the faces

connected to the collars
tied to the numbers
married to the hands
holding on to mine
and I saw unk and dookie
and baby bruh
chained to familiar nappy smiles
and noses
and I squeezed

this one holds two thousand
chants the Polish priest
as we cross the yard
after thirty minutes of security checks
metal detectors
infrared passes and written
and verbal agreements to not transport
weapons or other contraband
interrupted only by the reprocessing
of men in shackles and cuffs
and a rubber-gloved three-hundred-pound guard
lifting a senior noncitizen
out of a VA-supplied wheelchair
for a semidiscreet body cavity search

it is cold here
and the added draft created by the echo
of heavy steel doors
opening and closing
lowers the windchill factor
so I squeeze these baby brothas' hands
exchanging dap for unk and dookie

I squeeze for warmth
for all their loved ones on the outside

I squeeze out of guilt
ashamed of my own freedom
that I have taken for granted

what I cannot say with words
I squeeze into these cousins and uncles
and eyes
and they gather 'round and listen
like I'm some infamous escape artist
come to sing the freedom song
but I'm just a poet
and these are just words
not keys or dynamite
just words
not pardons

but if you rub them together
you can start a fire and right now
that's what we need
'cause it's cold here
it's damn cold on the inside
so I squeeze back
my tears
and we get warm

When I Can't Find the Words

When I can't find
the words
when there is nothing more
to say, I snap
I take wooden hostages
hold a blade to their necks
until they speak to me
revealing original names and secret passages to
their most beautiful selves
hidden deep inside the grain

In my dreams
when the trees begin to weep
when pine and walnut call my name
deny me shade, force splinters
into my tongue and feet
I hide in a dark room
force myself to view the world like a Rebel
through a lens
sneaking around like the wind
stealing frozen black and white moments
from strangers
locking them in windows and frames
pointing out the truth in the lies
all the time looking for the right words
verbs that run marathons with the sun

Sometimes I hear them coming
other times they leap out of my mouth
spill onto the page
translating themselves
while I stand guard and practice my alibi

Walk With Me Bashō
for Greg Pape

Tobacco fields are
oceans of sea turtle tongues
but my leaves are mute

Music underfoot
sounds like crumpled drafts launched toward
paper bed of leaves

Each flake mocks me, holds
hands with like minds pretending
to be a blank page

With each new bud, hope
with each fresh ink spill, promise
this word drought will end

Walk with me Bashō
teach me to draw one clear breath
and exhale water

Literary Patriarch
for Gurney Norman

Got my mamma's lips
but I dot my eyes like him
or so I'm told
She taught me how to stand
He taught me how to walk
into a classroom
up to a podium
and pretend
it was just the front porch
a collection of tree stumps
a circle of kin

Everything I know
about the Ohio River Valley
Appalachian literature
and postmodern community activism
I learned while riding
shotgun
into the mountains
marveling at his Mecca

Once
after a short hike
from Hindman to Hazard to Hazel Green
he pushed his glasses back on his nose
held up two chalkboard hands
and said

'What I see happening is this ... '
then proceeded to map out
concentric typographical circles
with grass roots
that ignored
continental and racial divides
and I believed
and have watched it all
unfold and spiral around me
just like he said it would

Some see
a silver sage
a bespectacled Daniel Boone
with his fountain pen cocked

I see
my literary father

After Charlotte Left George Ella's Party at Hindman

for the Appalachian Writers Workshop

Must have been some gathering last night
Widows and the long-legged must have filled
every corner in the room
nesting on floors and porches
hipbone to hipbone, thorax to thorax
crowding onto furniture, knees and laps
hanging from the ceiling

Did you see all them spider quilts
on the bridge this morning?
Some bodies was up all night
Must have stumbled down the hill
bobbing and weaving
still drunk off all that pure grain music
looked at the splayed metal fingers
holding up the wooden planks
straddling Troublesome Creek
and thought, damn!
class already started
sat down on the bank and wove this poem

My Poems Been Runnin'
They Mouths Again

you gotta be careful
what you say around children
'cause they are guaranteed to repeat it
when company comes

my poems are like that
speak ya mind
pour outcha heart
on a page
within earshot of black alphabet words
and they will run and tell somebody

let the ink and paper verses
you carried for nine months
or the rhymes born prematurely
hear what you covet
who you despise
where you buried the body
and they will betray you, for sure

I have learned I cannot trust
my poems
everybody knows
more about me and my family now
than I would ever tell a soul
my mother asked me to
stop tellin' family secrets

ain't nobody's business but ours
what goes on in this house

I tried to tell her
that it was not me
that the poems
been runnin' they mouths again
and maybe she should keep 'em for awhile
try 'n talk some sense into they heads

so she took 'em home one day
gathered them
in a room
like grandchildren
sat them on her lap
turned their pages
one by one

when I returned
she met me at the door
fear in her voice
anger in her eyes
you gotta change 'em
she said
why'd you let them say
such bad things
about people you say you love?
change the titles
take out that part about him being from Kentucky
and people calling him names

if my sister reads these poems
it will break her heart

I knew right then
that they had gone and done it
maybe even crossed the line
disrespectin' my mamma like that
and I promised to beat they ass
as soon as I got 'em home
I knew it would hurt me
more than it would hurt them

but Mamma said
nah, just talk to 'em
try 'n reason with 'em
ask 'em t' compromise
t' use some discretion 'bout
what they tell to who
'cause you never know who's listenin'
or who's just waitin' t' use
your own words
against ya

How to Bury a Dead Man

Greet family and friends warmly and with hugs
Sit cross-armed and -legged
Shed no tears
Offer no remarks or condolences
Listen carefully for music in the monotonous
beeping of the smoke detector
Consider it a subtle message from beyond

Ignore apocalyptic warnings accompanying
invitations to give your life over to Jesus
Smile quietly at the widow's strength
Contribute to her monument of silence
Recognize that she took a vow
when it really meant something
Uncross your arms and legs
Bite your tongue, but write this poem

Write Like a Dog

for Lois

My words lose focus, pages blur
every time the chorus of howls peppers the air
just ahead of a stampede of padded feet
bounding down three flights of wooden stairs
pausing only to sniff

If the notes in their song arc upward
I know an approaching siren will join them
its frequency unavailable to me
until it is within a few city blocks

If the music comes from their chests
I know they will race through the yard
all but take the back fence
and wail away until the air is free from strangers

I am training myself to bark like that
to really listen, to write it all down as soon
as I can hear the words
so I lick the page with my pencil
scratch for my songs and try to write like a dog

The Dozens
for the Cave Canem Fellows

Harlem's renaissance
swallowed minstrels, lynchings, then
gave us Langston Hughes

Margaret Walker
taught us with *Jubilee* to
write for our people

We still cool. Use words
like tools, seek the wisdom in
Gwendolyn's jewels

No word warrior
no champion of black poems
smiles like our Haki

Tsunami songstress
igniting sistah fire words
be be be Sonia

If a poem catch a
fire and a movement burns in
it be Baraka

Just like you, Gene, your
photos and words wear kufis,
crown east St. Louis

Cornelius and Toi
warn us, but forget their dogs
cave poemas

In dictionaries
next to pictures of Rita
it says, eloquence

If Lucille Clifton
inspired Affrilachia's lion
she be my grand muse

With all these poets, black
loving and paving the way
how can we not write

To all young poets
carrying on tradition
right on scribes, write on!

Crooked Letter Crooked Letter Eye
Humpback Humpback Eye
for Al Young

Before I could spell Mississippi
you had already escaped north
to the Great Lakes
journeyed west to watch the sun
challenge the ocean
its drunken stubbornness a mirror
for your busy typewriter keys

Before I could decipher my aunt's
Pig Latin, you and your Spanish
had already conquered Madrid
and pages and pages of other
unrhymed photogenic places
lifetimes away from the lazy verbs
of the Delta

When I discovered that time of day
and location were the only real differences
between Mamma's gospel music
and Daddy's blues
you and your velvet chops
had already divorced the microphone
translated every pure jazz note into verve
charged the air around you, for life

I imagine our fathers
tinkering with old cars
wiping sweat from their brows on oily rags
fingernails black with pride
stuck in a round conversation
yours offering mine this bit of wisdom

Sing a boy a word an' he'll spell all day
Teach him to write an' he'll 'member you
taller than you ever was

Memento
for Nikky Finney

There's something about the way
she numbers her years here

Not like a prisoner scratching a line
on a wall, counting down her sentence
but a visitor
intent on not overstaying her welcome

I hear it when she looks out over
those of us
who creep closer, stay longer
just to hear the poet woman speak

Right there, in between the poems
down under the words
you hear her say she can't stay forever
though she's not yet ready to leave

Not today, not tomorrow
but her leaving
is coming
She's already begun
to prepare
deciding what to leave behind
with each of us
something solid
particular to the journey we are on

a memento as distinct as the color orange
as personal as a hidden freckle

She's leaving, eventually
but we know she'll go slow
like her granny's molasses
just like she came
as simple as rice
as true and blue as indigo

Boonesborough
Fort Boonesborough, est. 1775

They whisper
from the monument's shadow
with bronze lips engraved
in raised letters
at the end of the litany of official
white adventurers
the first two
our Osiris and Isis, our Adam and Eve
axe-wielding pioneers
who helped blaze a trail with Boone
to this almost Eden
south of the Kentucky river

Nameless but not anonymous
this 'Negro' man and woman
our primordial parents
our blackened bluegrass beginnings
planted their hopes near the river bed
carved out a place in the wilderness
that would one day give birth
to little pockets of us
wherever the rivers creeked and branched

They whisper from the shadows
from the south face of this historic stone
quietly claiming their place in history
on land both stolen and fought for

Read, they say,
A year before this country
had enough woman in her hips
to give birth to a fight for freedom
we were already here
playing midwife to what would
one day be our state, too

Beacon

for Stephen Bishop, first guide & explorer of
Mammoth Cave, died June 15, 1859 in his 37th year

There was a time when adventurers
and curiosity seekers
from all over the world
rode for days by stagecoach and saddle
to follow a mysterious man
deep into the pitch black

Tall, dark, incandescent
slinging flaming cloth torches
into the distance
mood lighting
to show off the earth's inner beauty

His shadow and directions
bounced off wet, jagged ceilings and walls
His laughter echoed
and filled the cavernous corners
a warm beacon
as easy to follow as the hand-held
lard oil lamps

Today, he lies in state
beneath a borrowed tombstone
above the historic entrance
of this deep hollow ground
a mammoth cave as familiar to him

as the inside of his own mouth
with miles of trails as recognizable as
the underground river of veins
on the back of his hands

They traveled to see a trailblazer
They came to follow a dark man
with the power to shine light
on our unspoken subterranean fears

What better tool for abolition's sake
than a slave
leading the way into the depths
and out of our collective darkness

Great Day in Harlan
for Bill Turner

they stood there at the mouth
of shaft number five
like they were planted in the streets of Harlem
somewhere west of 125th and Lenox

lunch pails under their arms
hands clenched tightly in permanent fists
heads cocked like skilled musicians with pickaxes
and number nine shovels tucked in horn cases
or wrapped in velvet bags

coal dust soaking up the sun
backs straight, shoulders and chins up
listening to the music of their lives
muted by the syncopated rhythms of work

no prohibition against pride here
it's hard to look tall standing at the foot of a mountain
but if you gotta swing an axe, swing it like you wrote
the music, swing it like it got five strings
swing it like you diggin' coal

Blues Ridge

no mills, no mines
no mills, no mines
no means to make money
meet mortgages
manage marriages
maybe matriculate

no meals, no minds
no meals, no minds
means mountains
means many more may move
or meet makers
married to mountains
blue enough to make you sing

Meteorologist

... until justice rolls down like waters
and righteousness like a mighty stream –MLK, Jr.

I hope it rained all night
when a black man, his wife, their baby
and five children
were lynched
because They said he cursed
a white woman

I hope the thunder and lightning
washed out roads, caused flash floods
turned brooks and creeks
into angry rapids
every time an innocent black body
was lifted heavenward
by good white Christians
protecting the honor and chastity
of white girls and women
who might be offended
or rendered impure
if the naked eyes, long hard looks
or penetrating stares
of a black man happened their way

I hope it rains until racists
confront what they really fear
until truth finally convinces them
that color doesn't matter

I hope the thunder and lightning
wash out roads, cause flash floods
turn brooks and creeks
into angry rapids
    all night long

Whether they drown or are baptized
it won't wash these sins away

Theory of Relativity

To be in the Middle East
so close to Egypt and not
build a naked Arab pyramid
then pose for pictures
would have been un-American
Our peace officers have done much worse
than haze detainees
and sic dogs on grown men

Remember the waterlogged women and children
in Birmingham, police batons on their backs
German shepherds at their throats?

Where was the outrage, the horror
when Americans were lynching
black men all those years?
Who were those smiling faces
posing next to
charred and dismembered bodies
photos later used
as souvenirs and postcards?

Relatively speaking, it was not Wounded Knee
It didn't involve smallpox blankets
syphilis experiments
or any form of genocide

It was not Nagasaki
or even Vietnam

Relatively speaking, it was no worse
than flunking American History. Right?

Bread and Fruit

Singing his name in a tongue
he didn't understand
wishing him husband
she knew she'd never have
she found him in the dark
every night
rubbed his anger to sleep
gifted him with bread crumbs and dried fruit
liberated from above

Arms circling his back
cursing the chains that prevented him
from holding her
she rode and cried
rode and laughed
mocking the death that rode with them
mocking the strange pale ones
with stone eyes and hands
that passed her at knifepoint

She knelt and served
rubbed spilled honey on her breast
honey hardened by the ocean sun
that when set
would mix with saltwater tears
and free a lover
a deck away

Massage
for David Flores, Sr.

When Papa Flores hums
every sound in the room
disappears
following his ancient voice
I close my eyes and journey back

Turning my palms up
he enters my spirit through my fingertips

As I focus my breathing he crawls slowly
up my arms, locates the tension
between my shoulder blades
and squats down in the deep tissue

One by one he isolates the worries
I have tied to rocks stacked on
slumping shoulders
and rolls them down my arms
and out to sea

Lying there at the edge of the cliff
I listen and wait for the sound of crashing rocks
but hear only his humming
as he taps me lightly on the forehead
smiles and nods
pronouncing me fit to leave

Camel Conquers Eye of Needle

Enjoying the guilty pleasure
of owning something
even land
was in violation of
an eleventh or twelfth commandment
back then

I always felt blessed
to have even the simplest food, shelter, clothing
to be healthy enough to walk to a bus stop
while I dreamed of buying a good used car

I'm a new landowner now
The land is old, but my owning even a parcel of it
is new
It's not the acreage my great grandparents used to farm
before their grandchildren
developed a taste for the city then sold out

No tobacco, no barns, no pigs, no wells
not even close
but when I push my red Troy-Bilt lawnmower
back to the garage, sweat rolling off my brow
the salt in my smile is tempered by winters spent
walking the wealthy fringes
of the university's rolling estates
snow shovel over my shoulder
high-top sneakers over thin tube socks

Eclipsing even earlier seasons
spent mowing other people's lawns
raking other people's leaves
owning only the effort, the calluses, the anger
when my reward for a day's work
was only one dollar, a smug smile and a glass
of bitter lemonade

Today's salt, smile and satisfaction
are seasoned by four-plus decades
of paying rent, of being someone else's
miscellaneous extra income
car payment, college fund
or savings account

After spending the morning
on my hands and knees
pulling weeds in my own back yard
and now, looking out the window
at my grandson
wound up on Froot Loops
running in circles in the middle
of what surely seems like
forty acres to him
I feel abundantly rich
and already in the Kingdom

Ms. CegeNation

for Cori, Alexus, Alyvia, Isabella & Samantha

What do we tell our daughters
whose mothers or fathers are white?
who are equal parts Asian, Latina or black
when people and families can be so closed-minded
judgmental and unforgiving?

How can we thicken their opaque skin
hug them bulletproof
put steel rivets in their backbones
when all we can say is

> *Never apologize for who you are*
> *Never accept being labeled exotic*
> *Only make space for people in your life*
> *who are not afraid of your strength*
> *who understand your ethnic wealth*
> *who will show you constellations*
> *of rainbow-colored heroines*
> *and dare you to claim your own space*
> *in the sky*

What do we tell our daughters
whose identities, whose history
whose self-esteem won't fit neatly into a box?
Tell them

> *There are no accidents*

Urge them to live their lives
fully and with purpose
To smile at the face in the mirror
as if the whole world is watching
a newborn
breathe

Sunday Morning

I am still too country
to feel at home in a city's megachurch
more coliseum than cathedral
less temple than stadium
all theater
driven by charismatic ordained leading men
and the purses
of loyal devotees
seeking salvation

Morning streets crowded
with evangelical vans and buses
I eagerly trade my four lanes for two
rolling past heritage signs
crediting Irish craftsmen for rock fences
my grandfathers built
past the suburbs of Masterson, Bracktown
and Blackburn, another prison industrial complex

My prayer book opens as
manicured lawns become fields
lilac and honeysuckle gather at the edge of the road
filling the air with sweet psalms
welcoming, watching
nodding occasionally, the wind's willing witness

Estates become farms
rows of cornstalks and tobacco plants
are gathered for worship
There are families of trees out here
standing around in groves
providing shade for a small herd of heifers
and each other

At the edge of the asphalt, dirt and gravel driveways
more barns than houses
more horses than barns
    and only me

In the country the road is married to the land
wears the same hips as the creek branches
rides every hill like a daughter
on her daddy's knee

Out here, the sun is Lord
worshippers pray for rain
and they get up every morning
and go to church
in the field

Son Rise

At the intersection of Peachtree
and Auburn, between Park and Luckie Street
an Atlanta son rises before the tourists
and waits to be kissed by the light

At the foot of urban majesty
at the center of commerce
marble, steel and glass
scrape the sky
while e-business and Olympic residue
embrace a silent Sunday morning

Calvin Clark, married, with children
54, able-bodied but homeless
bloodshot eyes
reeking of alcohol he begs, no asks
passersby politely for a smoke
mumbles to me that he dreamed about
Kentucky last night and South Carolina
said it must have been the cigarettes
and that nicotine calling

I so much a boy of the bluegrass
that I am the color of tobacco and bourbon
am suddenly attentive
not believing in coincidences

I put my amateur photojournalism
on hold
join him on the stoop
trying not to stare at his
Tommy Hilfiger shoes
or his crusty unwashed face
equally out of place together

I offer him two dollars for breakfast
and five to take his picture
He accepts
apologizes for being needy
then volunteers that his mind
comes and goes
and sometimes he just acts a fool
but that he is not himself
didn't used to stutter
done eleven years on the inside
used to box and teach
used to paint too

Done three weeks in this park
been robbed three times
but didn't want to hurt nobody
sick 'n tired a hurt

All I did to them was pray for 'em
he says, figured they must need it
way more 'n me

Pointing upward, he says
I talked to Him last night
and He said
   eva thang gonna be all right
so I ain't givin' up
I ain't neva givin' up

Black Leprechauns
Derry, Northern Ireland

I was surprised to see Uncle Remus hanging
on the wall in a pub in Northern Ireland
Another great American export met me
halfway across the world in a bar named after
Peadar O'Donnell, a working-class revolutionary

A bar that features flags from Corsica
Catalonia and the Basque region
in a neighbourhood that understands oppression
a former battleground for Irish Catholic civil rights
should be posting pictures of Huey Newton
and Fred Hampton, not a subservient Uncle Tom
Angela Davis, fist high, crowned in a defiant Afro
not Aunt Jemima in a handkerchief

I didn't want to find Uncle Remus
eyes wide and grinning, hanging on the wall
in a pub in Ireland
where the favourite drink
is the colour of my mother
and every chance encounter the flavour
of a family reunion

I was not looking for Uncle Remus
Uncle Tom or Uncle Sam
but I guess when you're really really good
at something
the whole world will notice

Spit Shine

In Houston, at the George Bush International airport
the smiling faces
on the surface of the cowboy boots
are a leathery brown
los hermanos whisper shots
of Español left and right
izquierda y derecha
in between perfectly enunciated
'how are you today sir'
smiles

Suits glance down, past floating feet
and back to the *Times* or the *Wall Street Journal*
frowning at stock quotes
oblivious to the rhythmic percussion
of the rag and brush

In Louisville, in the lobby of the Brown Hotel
the shoeshine stand is empty
yet still bustling with the ghosts
of invisible black men
ageless and grinning
who tip their hats politely
palms up, eyes down
silently signaling submission
to Italian leather wingtips

Somewhere a minstrel is singing
a familiar tune to cooks
valets, chauffeurs and the wait staff

To shine in America
you only need two polishes
one brown
one black

Silent Witness

7:00 A.M.
A screaming woman
interrupts my paper-and-pencil breakfast
slapping the innocence of morning
flush on the cheeks
Barefoot, I step out on the landing
a lone black sentinel

Truck tires bruise the parking lot
Legs swallow stairs whole
two and three at a time
He knocks first with a fist
then his boot becomes a key
Falling, breaking lamps jerk
like flashbulbs, like lightning captured
behind curtain edges
In the middle of the thunder
he becomes the new front door
striking a King Kong pose

Center stage
he looks up to see me
shirtless, barefoot, arms crossed
a witness
and slows his roll

Anger muted, he winds himself backward
down the staircase
exchanging *you betta*s and *I'm gonna*s
for her *leave me alone*s

As he pulls out of the parking lot
he shoots an accusatory look in my direction
and I wonder *why* this is none of my business

Fetal Position

We swap scars
exchange rememberings
your C-section and an ugly secret
for the extra lifeline that snakes
the ocean of my palm

You force a smile
your pain seeps out
fogging the mood in the room

You put your thumb
in your mouth
seeking the comfort only mothers
and milk can provide

For a moment, the time
it takes a butterfly to scream,
you are a little girl again
bubbling with innocence
too young to say uncle
too damaged to crayon rape

Curled up there
inside yourself
I hear you wish you
had never been born

Watching you cry
even my
water   breaks

Hollow
for Aunt Minnie

What do you say
when a loved one brings
death home for dinner
and introduces her
like a lesbian lover
an interracial romance
or some other traditionally
unwelcome guest
that might become more palatable
by dessert
after twenty questions
and forced
but polite
conversation?

How do you pretend
that the sight
of post-chemo
hollowness
and a pillowcase full of hair
is normal
as you fight not to stare
search the ceiling tiles
and carpet
for lighthearted
icebreakers

and beg your own eyes
to lie?

What
do you say?

You say, I love you

You say, your prayers

And you swallow
every   good   bye
real   slow

Last Writes: A Requiem for Mamma

i.

this is the first morning i've run
since we gave her to the ground
this is the first dirt i've sprinkled
since i walked out of the church
after finding quiet in my own season of tears

i follow the creek around the road
to a cemetery
i know the peace i'm seeking
is somewhere among the granite
i know i will hajj here every morning at sunrise
to look for lessons
chiseled in stone

clyde and eliza
john and raye
russell and thelma
robert and pearl
rows and rows of tutors
hugging the edge of the cobblestone path
and each other

i have traveled
to these quiet pennsylvania hills
to get lost, to be invisible
to hide in a forest of poets

i don't tell them
i'm here to bury a loved one
i don't tell them
i'm here to say goodbye to my mother

ii.
a banner announcing
50% off plots purchased now   an empty vase

styrofoam crosses hidden
by crooked flags   a fallen concrete bench

every shade and texture of gray
cast in   rows and rows of granite

one day i will return here
and see nothing but   flowers

iii.
these stones, my father's stoic cousins,
help me recall the gentle hand
he placed on my shoulder
at her homegoing
there were no words
i thought he said nothing
they say i wasn't listening

iv.
water's exact path and speed
are barely discernable
until it encounters   a rock
only then does it write its course

choose a new path
invite this stubborn obstacle's roughness
into a seductive duel
that makes all rocks smaller   over time

v.
i put on a white cotton tee
and exit the building
the brisk morning air reminds me
to draw deep clean breaths
and begin again

when the lavender wildflowers
dance in the weeds at the edge of the road
i shorten my stride, slow to a walk and
pick up three black rocks

this will be my fourth morning
at hillview cemetery
i left my family
and a fresh grave back in kentucky
on the other side of these appalachian hills

maybe i come here out of guilt, maybe i come here
to bury something in me, to dig myself out of a hole
maybe this is as close to home as i can get

by now my mountain mornings
have fallen into a pattern
at dawn, i follow one road across two bridges
the same creek
and deposit gifts of stone into still water

in my mind, i am laying the foundation
for an underwater
pyramid

i circle each field of monuments
first at a reverential pace
then briskly like a parade march

hannah and hiram hawk, first row, second field
willard shakespeare, back row, third field
the smooth black kemp family obelisk
somewhere in the middle

the tiny apple-shaped headstones
of the three smith children
given back to earth
before breathing even five months
the youngest only nine days

i circle these stones
i gather and gift these rocks
i cross these bridges, this creek again and again
singing my mother's name
clinging to her with both hands
praying for permission
to let go

vi.
this morning is the coldest yet
collecting my gifts, crossing the road at the bridge
i imagine the asphalt is water
as i wade through two quiet lanes

depositing the rocks
i shift my focus to a family of ducks
wading in the shadows
my eyes follow them as each ball
of feathers tests its independence
under the watchful gaze of an emerald-crowned
guide leading them upstream
from behind

they swim through the still water
under me and the bridge

after counting and recounting and counting again
my eyes cannot leave the seven of them
even when they disappear
even when the surface ripples they create
return to rest

on the way up the hill
i think about the seven deep scars
on the terracotta figure in my room
the weight of children
clinging to her back
   and for the first time
   imagine my siblings have joined me on this hajj

circling the stone fields
for what feels like the last time
our eyes scan the stones like a page
pausing on names and phrases
as though we're reading a favorite poem

vii.

i run around the last field
like i did when we were children
when i stop to collect my breath
i add the rock in my shoe
to the seven white ones i discovered
while circling today's stones

for the first time this week, i turn my back
walk barefoot to the creek
line up the rocks by size and birth order
cradle and squeeze each one
hoping to slow, if not stop, the passing of time
i whisper a prayer with each letting go
for wanda
    debra
    brenda
    cecil
    karla
    sonya
    and me

i offer the last stone and a kiss as a gift
run all the way home
laughing, smiling
and in tears

Haiku for Nikki

watermelon seeds
when swallowed, bloom in nine moons
challenge gravity

protective fathers
who tell the lie about storks
still can't sleep at night

nikki's tiny frame
is young, but strong enough to
carry an ocean

hearing that daughter's
water broke, I shed a tear
pray the child be quick

grandfatherhood makes
gray hairs, bald head and bad knees
easy to swallow

my joints always ache
before it rains, I will be
all knees if it storms

after nine months of study
childbirth is the entrance exam
to a life of worry

an eight-pound one-ounce
twenty-and-a-half inch
baby boy arrives

when I close my eyes
I see his mamma squinting
counting fingers, toes

La Arquitectura
for Michaele

i dreamed god sent me a woman
who was blind, to teach me how
to really see
a woman with the power of the sun
harnessed in tiny freckles
planted like butterfly kisses upon her face

we move through an exhibit
like Alvin Ailey disciples
choreographing a signature waltz
or an underwater tango
we move like dolphins
joined at the fin

don't taste this art with a stranger, I say
tell me what you hear

closing the distance between us, she smiles
slow and easy, like the day wakes
parts her lips like an eye opens, and says
i hear your heartbeat
i hear your smile and sincerity
i hear a southern boy's quiet confidence, like
Harriet Tubman looking back
after crossing number three hundred

or the sound an architect makes
when she looks at a pile of bricks
and sees only its potential

spidering her fingers to my mouth, she says
resist the urge to describe the texture
and basic composition on the wall
tell me about the temperature
of the piece, pretend i'm only interested
in what's beneath the surface
or what the artist was thinking, help me see
the light on the faces of others
when they stop to whisper
are they enraptured? confused? curious?

they're all smiling, i say
but they're not looking at the walls
they're looking at you … and the temperature?
    it is smoldering

she laughs and says
then i must look as incredible as i feel
swimming next to you
or we're standing here without clothing
possibly deserving all this attention

oh yes, i assure her, we are most definitely naked
everyone here can see right through us
an easy thing
when you have nothing to hide

but i do, she says,
they can't see my memories
they can't see where i go when i surrender
to sleep at night

maybe they remember your touch
from their dreams, as i do
maybe in you and your works they see the Orishas
and that is comfort enough

we tread water together, quietly
considering the possibilities

listen, she says
no, really listen

i close my eyes
and find her fingertips
waiting for me
in the dark

Voyeur

I like to see a city
before she's fully dressed
sticky wet dew in the corner of her eyes
just before fog
has melted away last night's makeup
and all her pretenses, but not the scent
of our adventures

I never feel I know a place
until I've spent a full night with her
watched her surrender to sleep or fatigue
after locking all the doors
pulling the blinds down and
the sheets and covers back

Southern cities prop open their windows at night
discard their silks and lace, preferring cotton
or nothing
to come between them and the evening breeze

You haven't seen a city
until you've watched her sleep at night
and kissed her full on the lips
just before she wakes

Cincinnati

Like the last drag on the last
menthol, night holds her breath
then exhales a skyline shrouded
in blue darkness

Before the sun comes, the weight of day
is still in her womb, a blanket so warm
even the sirens feign sleep

Any minute now, the sky will surrender
to time clocks, empty streets and sidewalks
will stretch, yawn, then boil over with
eight-plus hours of caffeine-driven commerce

But right now I am savoring
the remaining dark's kiss
the calm, the only thing I really own
before she bites the stillness
yanking the welcome mat
from under my feet

He Who Sleeps Alone

This was not always his name
Once it was
    he who loves too much
    he who loves too many
    he who cannot choose
The truth is
he was afraid to be alone
though he lived only to be by himself

Truth is, away from her, away from them
was the only time he could fool around   with words

At first he adored the silence, his own private space
living near the railroad tracks, in the path of airports
next to the highway, made him feel at home

Truth is, he was afraid of empty beds and quiet houses
Tiny apartments for large poor families
meant sharing everything, even the covers

Truth is, the hum of the TV, the books, magazines,
newspapers, remote controls, empty plates and cups
especially in hotel rooms, help fill up the empty spaces
and in the dark without glasses
they almost resemble   her

Black Box

An empty tobacco barn   the pinhole camera we
                            made from a cigar box

hotel rooms after finally
surrendering to exhaustion   a coal mine

behind the curtain where
sunburned negatives blink   and drowning images are
                                rescued from water

that tender space filled with
all my childhood memories   the last classroom
                                I'll ever teach in

these are the only real places
where light closes her eyes   and sleeps

Anniversary
for the Affrilachian Poets

Ten thousand pages later
this herd of buffalo
still gathers
on Affrilachian shores
to taste each other's ink
be warmed
by smoldering embers
of coal
black voices

Navigating by pencil, at night
we plot courses
through Seattles
Chicagos and New Yorks
but we are anchored here
in this cast iron skillet
called Kentucky
our lives sewn
together, hand stitched
by old fingers
knowing eyes
who saw the all-cotton
quilt
in us
when we were only
thread

Wings

Throwing salt, spitting on brooms
shaking a dropped spoon or fork to ward off
uninvited guests
Aunt Helen always warned
that death would come in threes
or for someone close
if she dreamed about a ghostly rider
on a pale horse

She refused to believe
that God would let lowly man
walk on the moon
creating my first conspiracy theory
and a life of paranoia

I look closely at random feathers
cast secret backward glances into makeshift mirrors
speak to the presence and protection she promised
when streetlights suddenly go dim or flicker

When my car hydroplanes and spins
across four lanes of traffic
showing me a long slow look at the world
and lands inches away from a concrete median
undisturbed, unscratched, and still pointed
in the right direction,
I believe

ACKNOWLEDGMENTS

Earlier versions of the following poems were previously published in:

BOOKS
A Kentucky Christmas, 'Too Wise Men'

The Kentucky Anthology: Two Hundred Years of Writing in the Bluegrass State, 'View Finder'

Role Call: A Generational Anthology of Social & Political Black Literature & Art, 'Son Rise'

Tobacco: A Literary Anthology, 'View Finder'

Spirit & Flame: An Anthology of Contemporary African American Poetry, 'Bread Fruit'

JOURNALS
Wind, 'Canning Memories'

Kudzu, 'Literary Patriarch' / 'After Charlotte Left George Ella's Party at Hindman' / 'Enough' / 'Creek Philosophy' / 'Canning Memories' / 'Glutton' / 'Blues Ridge'

Appalachian Heritage, 'Literary Patriarch'

The Round Table, 'View Finder'

SNReview, 'Altitude Adjustment' / 'Enough' / 'Why We Keep Plants' / 'Glutton' / 'Writes of Passage'

Chrysanthemum, 'He Who Sleeps Alone'

ABOUT THE AUTHOR

FRANK X WALKER is a native of Danville, Kentucky, and the author of two previous books of poetry: *Affrilachia* (Old Cove Press, 2000) and *Buffalo Dance: The Journey of York* (University Press of Kentucky, 2003). He was awarded the 2005 Lannan Foundation Literary Fellowship for Poetry. In 2004, he received the Lillian Smith Book Award for *Buffalo Dance*. A founding member of the Affrilachian Poets and a Cave Canem Fellow, Walker served as consulting producer of the documentary *Coal Black Voices* (Media Working Group, 2001). He lives in Lexington, Kentucky.